IN

The

G000161811

A book and guide to

... Companion

... Church Teaching

by

DENIS E. TAYLOR

lately Dean of Brisbane

RELIGIOUS AND MORAL EDUCATION PRESS
An Imprint of Arnold-Wheaton

Printed in Great Britain by
A. Wheaton & Co. Ltd, Exeter

ISBN 0 08-030631-4 flexi
ISBN 0 08-030632-2 hard

FOREWORD

By the former Bishop of St Andrews

A BOOK is like a child. After it is conceived in its author's mind it remains hidden and secret while it slowly takes shape, but on its appearance in the world it assumes an independent life of its own, its begetter looking on with wistful hope, trusting that it may find a welcome and have a prosperous life.

Next to the privilege of being a father is the honour of being a godfather; and I am proud to stand sponsor for this little book which is now in your hands. Without doubt it will keep the 'promises' which are involved in its appearance. It is on the greatest of all subjects, on which our immortal well-being depends, and will teach its readers (old as well as young) how to 'draw near'.

Perhaps the highest praise I can give to it is to say that it is a characteristic product of its author, and he is well qualified to write it. As he grows older (like Wordsworth's 'Happy Warrior') he keeps undimmed in his mind the experience of youth; and now, with the wisdom of the mature, can speak with understanding to the heart of the young.

LUMSDEN BARKWAY

ACKNOWLEDGEMENTS

The Order for Holy Communion Rite B from The Alternative Service Book 1980 is © The Central Board of Finance of the Church of England, 1980, and is reproduced with permission. The Te Deum, which is © International Consultation on English Text, and Bless the Lord, which is a scriptural canticle and derives from the Daily Office of the Joint Liturgical Group (of Churches in Great Britain), are reproduced with permission.

Extracts from Psalms 8, 51 and 104, from *The Psalms: A New Translation for Worship*, Copyright © English text 1976, 1977 David L. Frost, John A. Emerton and Andrew A. Macintosh, Copyright © Pointing 1976, 1977 Wm Collins Sons & Co. Ltd, are reproduced by permission of Collins Liturgical Publications.

Extracts from the New English Bible, Second Edition, Copyright © 1970, are reproduced by permission of Oxford and Cambridge University Presses.

The prayer beginning 'We thank you, heavenly Father, ...' on page 107 has been adapted from a prayer in the Church of Scotland *Book of Common Order* (1940) and is reproduced by permission of Saint Andrew Press.

The prayer beginning 'We thank you, Lord, ...' on page 107 is from *The Methodist Service Book 1975* and is used by permission.

CONTENTS

IN HIS PRESENCE

PART I: PRAYER

EACH NEW DAY

'I am with you alway.'

At the beginning of a new day our aim is to offer to God all that lies ahead and to ask for his help and for the knowledge that he is with us, present beside us all the time. For he *is* always with us, though we, busy with the day's work and cares, may often forget him.

On the morning before the battle of Edgehill, the Cavalier Sir Jacob Astley prayed:

> Lord, I shall be very busy this day.
> If I forget thee,
> Do not thou forget me.

At the start of the new day, then let us offer it to our Father, praying above all that we may have a clear sense of his presence.

> Closer is he than breathing and
> nearer than hands and feet.

Kneel. Remember that our Lord is very near. Say reverently and thoughtfully:

In the name of the Father, and of the Son, and of the Holy Spirit.

Thank God for the rest and safety of the night now past, for health and powers renewed. Offer to God the day that is beginning:

**Blessed Lord, I thank you for rest and safety
   through the hours of night.
For this new day in which to serve you,
For powers of mind and body made new once more,
I worship and adore your glorious name.**

Praise and adore God, using these verses from the Te Deum:

**You are God and we praise you:
   you are the Lord and we acclaim you;
you are the eternal Father:
   all creation worships you.
To you all angels, all the powers of heaven:
   cherubim and seraphim sing in endless praise,
Holy holy holy Lord, God of power and might:
   heaven and earth are full of your glory.
Throughout the world the holy Church acclaims you:
   Father of majesty unbounded;
your true and only Son, worthy of all worship:
   and the Holy Spirit, advocate and guide.
You, Christ, are the King of glory:
   the eternal Son of the Father.**

PRAYERS

Day by day we bless you:
   we praise your name for ever.
Keep us today, Lord, from all sin:
   have mercy on us, Lord, have mercy.
Lord, show us your love and mercy:
   for we put our trust in you.
In you, Lord, is our hope:
   let us not be confounded at the end.

Ask for help in the coming day:

Most Holy Jesus, Friend and Master, you are ever near; keep me today from sin in all I think and do and say.

Help me to know that you are by my side to give me strength when I am tempted, and wisdom when I am puzzled or in doubt.

Blessed Lord, I offer this day to you. May everything that I do be to your glory and reflect your love. Help me to know that in doing my work I am doing your will, and that in serving others, I am serving you.

In this way, may I grow closer to you, my Master and my Friend.

Try to be up in time to do some of your work of Intercession. Turn to pages 20 to 26 for this.

Our Father ... Amen.

May the Grace of our Lord Jesus Christ, and the Love of God, and the fellowship of the Holy Spirit, be with me in all I do this day and for evermore. Amen.

THE PARTS OF PRAYER

Each night our private prayers should be modelled like this:

ADORATION First, love, adore and praise God in whom we live and move, and have our being. Praise him for his noble acts, praise him for his excellent greatness. Adore him for Jesus Christ. Love him because he first loved us and gave himself for us.

CONFESSION A sense of all that God is and all he does for us at once brings home our own unworthiness, how often we fail to live up even to our own ideals, how poor our fight against temptation, how weak our efforts to pray better, how uncostly our work for others and for our Lord. So we confess these our sins to God, and ask forgiveness.

THANKSGIVING The knowledge that when we are truly sorry and really mean to do better, we are forgiven makes thankfulness well up in our hearts, and we set ourselves to remember our many blessings—health, home, food, work, friends, play, our Church, all the joy of being alive—and we return thanks to God our Father.

SUPPLICATION Having adored God, having confessed our sinfulness, having thanked him for all his goodness and loving-kindness, then and then only we ask for more blessings. We make our supplications first for the needs of others, for great causes, for friends and for enemies. These are our Intercessions. Afterwards we pray for ourselves—we tell God our hopes, our joys, our fears, our desires, our needs. These are our Petitions.

Such prayers are A-C-T-S indeed,

true ACTS of worship.

Kneel. Remember that our Lord is very near. Say reverently and thoughtfully:

In the name of the Father, and of the Son, and of the Holy Spirit.

Be very still. Let the rush and hurry of the day die away as you kneel in silence in his presence. Think of the wonder and majesty of God the Creator of this universe, of earth and sea, of stars and illimitable space. Try to express your wonder and love.

Adoration

Blessed are you, Lord God, from of old and for ever. Yours, Lord, is the greatness, the power, the glory, the splendour and the majesty; for everything in heaven and on earth is yours; yours is the sovereignty and you are exalted over all as head. Wealth and honour come from you; you rule over all ... And now, we give you thanks, our God, and praise your glorious name.

I will bless the Lord continually:
his praise shall be always in my mouth.

Jesu, my Lord, I thee adore.
O make me love thee more and more.

(Often use other words of adoration. Some are given on page 16.)

PRAYERS

Confession

Think back over the day. What good have you left undone? Have you said or done anything wrong or mean? Sometimes use the questions for self-examination on page 65. Always do this before Communion. When you have thought back carefully over the day, tell God where you have failed.

Almighty God, our heavenly Father, I have sinned against you and against my fellow men, in thought and word and deed, through negligence, through weakness, through my own deliberate fault. Especially I have failed in these ways ... I am truly sorry and repent of all my sins. For the sake of your Son Jesus Christ, who died for us, forgive me all that is past; and grant that I may serve you in newness of life; to the glory of your name. Amen.

Sometimes you may like to express special penitence in the solemn words of Psalm 51.

Have mercy on me, O God, in your enduring goodness:
> **according to the fullness of your compassion blot out my offences.**

Wash me thoroughly from my wickedness:
> **and cleanse me from my sin.**

For I acknowledge my rebellion:
> **and my sin is ever before me.**

Create in me a clean heart, O God:
> **and renew a right spirit within me.**

Pray earnestly in your own words for forgiveness.

13

Thanksgiving

Not only does God forgive our sins when we repent, and for this we should thank him gladly, but our life is full of blessings. Health, home, food, friends are only a few, and there is the greatest blessing of all— the friendship of our Lord Jesus Christ. These suggestions may remind you of blessings for which to thank God:

Health	Work	Clothing
Parents	Home	Food
My Church	Friends, especially	
Good times, especially	Beauty in God's handiwork, e.g. country, garden, sea	
Help in temptation, especially	Beauty in man's handiwork, e.g. music, painting, books	

When you have considered, then thank God with all your heart:

Almighty and everlasting God, I praise and thank you for all your countless goodness and mercies towards me. Especially I thank you for ... Help me to be truly thankful for these and for all your good gifts by giving myself to your service and by walking before you in holiness and righteousness all my days; through Jesus Christ our Lord, to whom with you and the Holy Spirit be all honour and glory, for ever and ever. Amen.

PRAYERS

Supplication

There are, of course, some special people and needs you will wish to pray for every night:

Father .... Mother ....

Husband or Wife ....

Home, special difficulties .... needs ....

Brothers .... Sisters ....

Special friends ....

Relations ....

Anyone seriously ill or dying ....

One who has died ....

My own needs and hopes ....

Turn to your Intercession Notes for each day of the week, pages 20 to 26.

Sum up your Adoration, Confession, Thanksgiving and Supplication in our Lord's own words:

Our Father...

Into your hands, O Lord, I commend myself and all for whom I have prayed tonight. Keep us in your loving care and bless us all, I pray. Amen.

ACTS OF ADORATION

'O praise ye the Lord.'

Here are some glorious words with which to offer God your praise.

Holy, holy, holy Lord, God of power and might, heaven and earth are full of your glory. Hosanna in the highest.

Glory to the Father and to the Son and to the Holy Spirit; as it was in the beginning, is now, and shall be for ever. Amen.

Bless the Lord, the God of our fathers:
   sing his praise and exalt him for ever.
Bless his holy and glorious name:
   sing his praise and exalt him for ever.
Bless him in his holy and glorious temple:
   sing his praise and exalt him for ever.
Bless him on the throne of his kingdom:
   sing his praise and exalt him for ever.
Bless him in the heights of heaven:
   sing his praise and exalt him for ever.
Bless the Father, the Son and the Holy Spirit:
   sing his praise and exalt him for ever.

Now to him who is able to do immeasurably more than all we can ask or conceive, by the power which is at work among us, to him be glory in the Church and in Christ Jesus throughout all ages. Amen.

O Lord our Governor:
    how glorious is your name in all the earth!
When I consider your heavens, the work of your
    fingers:
    the moon and the stars which you have set in order,
what is man, that you should be mindful of him:
    or the son of man that you should care for him?
Yet you have made him little less than a god:
    and have crowned him with glory and honour.
O Lord our Governor:
    how glorious is your name in all the earth.

Psalm 8

Bless the Lord, O my soul:
    O Lord my God, how great you are!
Clothed with majesty and honour:
    wrapped in light as in a garment.
I will sing to the Lord as long as I live:
    I will praise my God while I have any being.
May my meditation be pleasing to him:
    for my joy shall be in the Lord.

Psalm 104

Our hymn-books contain many magnificent acts of praise. Use these sometimes in your private prayers, e.g.

Holy, holy, holy, Lord God Almighty

and

My God, how wonderful thou art.

A SCHEME OF INTERCESSION

To pray for others, that is, to intercede, is a most important work. It is real work, hard work, service of the highest order.

If we pray only for ourselves and, maybe, our little circle, our prayers are *really* selfish. How tired we get of folk who can talk only about themselves! We do not want God to feel like that about us.

There is service and adventure in learning to take your part in the prayer work of the Church. You will find it makes your prayers more interesting and satisfying. You *know* you have done something useful and important.

But it is not easy. There are many difficulties, such as wandering thoughts, and your own weariness at bedtime. Why not make it your habit to drop in to your church for ten minutes on your way home from work every day to do this other work? If you do not pass near enough for that, could you not make your prayer time immediately after your meal, before going out for the evening?

Above all perseverance is needed. The Devil will try hard to break down any good habit you build up—he will put many difficulties in the way.

Remember that Jesus told us to go on praying and not grow weary of trying. He reminded us that perseverance in prayer is rewarded when he told of the widow who cried to an unjust judge for justice day after day, until the man at last granted her request because he was so thoroughly sick of her! Imagine our Lord likening himself to an unjust judge! But there are several stories Jesus told with a twinkle in his eye. One of these was on this subject of persevering in intercession—about the man who needed bread for a belated traveller and went to knock up a neighbour, already in bed, to borrow a loaf. He went on shouting for it till the neighbour just *had* to get up and give it. We are to persevere with our prayers.

Prayer is work. Work needs method.

On the next pages there is a scheme for Intercession arranged over the days of the week. Without an ordered scheme you are bound to forget much for which you should be praying. Hence this scheme for each day of the week and space to add your own notes.

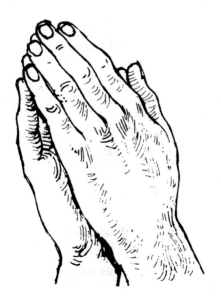

A PRAYER NOTEBOOK

SUNDAY—The Church of God

Sunday is the weekly commemoration of the rising of Christ from the tomb, to live and reign for evermore. The Church carries on his work.

Pray for

Your Bishop(s).   Your own parish clergy.

Members of your congregation, especially ....
....

Church workers—choir, Sunday-school teachers, sidesmen, servers, wardens, vestry, ladies' guild members, etc., especially ....

More priests. Remember the need for more manpower at home and overseas. For any thinking of ordination ....

The world-wide Church. Any need (e.g., unity, greater faith, converting the indifferent) ....
....

Any approaching great world event affecting the whole Church ....

That Christians may learn to give generously of their money and time in God's service.

That priests and lay people may strive to bring those outside who never worship into membership.

MONDAY—**The Church Overseas**

Pause to remember that but for the missionary zeal of the Apostles and early Christians we should have been left in paganism and fear. A first duty of a Christian is to win others to Christ. Thank God for the heroism of missionaries and that in most lands today there is a strong indigenous Church.

Pray for

Any missionary you know personally ....

Mission priests, doctors, nurses, teachers, agriculturalists, carpenters and mechanics, especially ....

The people among whom they work ... that they may have faith and courage to overcome opposition of family or neighbours in accepting Christ.

Indigenous priests, catechists, teachers, that they may give a fine witness among their own people.

The missionary societies' home headquarters.

Removal of colour barriers so that racial segregation and hatred may be overcome.

Churchpeople to understand still better and care more for the world mission of the Church.

(If you know little about the great work overseas ask the clergy for the monthly papers published by all missionary societies.)

TUESDAY—The Nations

Think of the events which are in the news, international problems, racial difficulties, peoples striving for independence, etc., etc. Bring to God the happenings which seem to you most urgent or dangerous and pray that God's will may be done.

Pray for

The United Nations, that it may build true fellowship between the nations.

The hungry in many lands.

Our own statesmen, especially ....

Leaders of other lands, especially ....

The people in lands without political freedom ......
....

Any who lead in the struggle for freedom ....

Christians persecuted for their religion or politics, or in fear or want, especially ....

Clubs and Fellowships

Pray for

Any club, association or fellowship, youth or adult, to which you belong—sporting, trade unionist, political, cultural or religious.

Members, especially ....

Chaplain ....

Particular needs or problems ....

WEDNESDAY—Earners and Industry

Pray for

Your office, shop or factory friends ....

The head, and others in authority ....

Those working in difficult, dangerous, or unhealthy conditions.

(If you do not know any personally, pray for miners, seamen, iron workers at blast furnaces, etc., those on night shift.)

Any unemployed or in money difficulties ....

Any unhappy in their jobs ....

Anyone unpopular ....

Difficulties at work ....

Schools, Colleges and Universities

Pray for

Your school, college or university ....

Your friends, especially ....

Teachers, lecturers, that they may inspire a love of the Christian faith, and appreciation of beauty, truth and real goodness ....

All keen young Churchpeople to see in teaching a great field of service for Christ ....

Any thinking of teaching, especially ....

THURSDAY—The Lonely and Old

Thursday is the day of Christ's lonely temptation in the Garden of Gethsemane.

Pray for

The lonely, particularly old people who have no one to care for and love them, especially ....
....

Thursday was also the day of Christ's Ascension to Heaven.

Thank God for the triumph of Jesus.

The Nation and Commonwealth

Pray for

Any part of the Commonwealth you know ....

Any Commonwealth problem (e.g., racial unity, political independence) ....

The Sovereign and Royal Family ....

The Prime Minister ....

Any M.P., local councillor, or magistrate, especially
....

Urgent local or national questions (e.g., housing, crime, etc.) ....

All the nations of the Commonwealth to be a power for peace throughout the world.

FRIDAY—**All Who Need Christ's Love**

Friday is the day of the Crucifixion of Jesus.

Pray for

A clearer realization of God's great love for us—love so great that he was willing to die for us.

Greater willingness to work for God.

Unbelievers—any you know who seldom or never worship God, especially ....

(Perhaps someone in your office or home.)

Children without parents or home or religion, especially ....

Pray for

Doctors and nurses, especially ....

(Think of them in consulting room and hospital. Remember by name any you know.)

Sufferers. Any ill or suffering person you know. Lift them up to our Lord who loves them and suffered for all. Pray for each by name ....

Old people, especially ....
Homes for the aged, especially ....

(If you do not know any orphanages, rescue homes, hostels, or homes for old folk, ask your clergy to get someone along to talk about them. Much good work is little known. Much help is needed.)

Pray for

The Faithful departed, especially ....

SATURDAY—The Church at Home

Pray for

More manpower.

(Think of the inadequacy of one priest to thousands of people. Pray that more men will feel the call to the priesthood. They may not be conscious that God is calling them. Your prayers may help them realize.)

Pray for

More women workers, as missionaries, nurses, teachers, youth leaders, community-centre workers, deaconesses or Sunday-school teachers.

(Pray for any whom you think God might use in these ways. Perhaps he wants you?)

Pray that

Churchpeople may rise to the challenge to bring the Church to new housing areas. For this work in your diocese.

Pray for

Any special project in your own congregation ....
....
Sunday schools ....
Efforts to reach young people who attend no church
....
Any preparing for Confirmation, especially ....
....

(Are you making your Communion tomorrow? Turn to page 57.)

PART II: THE CHURCH

WHAT IS THE CHURCH?

What is the Church?   A Society—a divine Society because founded by Jesus Christ. Whitsunday is called the Birthday of the Church.

What is the Church for?   To carry on what Jesus began—to teach people the goodness, holiness and love of God and his purpose for men; to restore the relationship between God and man broken by man's disobedience which we call sin. The Church is to be the family of God's people, uniting them in worship and in work to set up his reign of justice and love, and helping them to bear witness to him by the quality of their lives.

How do we become members?   Entrance to the Church is by Baptism, in which a person is made a member of Christ, the child of God and an inheritor of the Kingdom of Heaven.

What do members try to do?   *Renounce*, that is, have nothing to do with anything evil, mean or second rate; *believe* and be tremendously happy about our Christian faith; *keep* God's holy will and commandments made plain through the Bible, the teaching of the Church, and our conscience; be fellow-workers with Jesus in spreading kindness and joy, setting up the reign of God on earth, his 'kingdom' of goodness and love; join together to worship and adore our Creator, the God 'Who made and loveth all'. Members try by prayer, the Sacraments, self-discipline and service to grow in the knowledge and love of Jesus.

27

What does the Church do for her members? Calls them together for worship; is the channel whereby God strengthens them for the difficulties and temptations of life by giving them the Holy Spirit in Baptism and Confirmation; refreshes them constantly through the Sacrament of the Body and Blood of Christ.

Teaches them about God, his intentions for men and their eternal destiny; gives them special help at the crossroads of life, e.g., marriage, illness; acts as a channel whereby the repentant receive forgiveness; joins them in a happy fellowship, the Church, an army pledged to carry on the work Christ began.

The Church includes not only her members in this world, the Church Militant here on earth (militant means fighting, i.e., waging war against sin and evil); but also those who have passed on to the life beyond. They are called the Church Expectant (i.e., waiting while being made perfect) and the Church Triumphant in Heaven.

Who are the Church's ministers? The Church has a threefold ministry: bishops, priests and deacons. A man is made deacon first, and may not celebrate Holy Communion, pronounce Absolution nor give the Blessing. After one year as deacon he is ordained priest and can exercise every function of the Ministry except those reserved for bishops (following the example of the Apostles).

Bishops only may administer Confirmation (see Acts 8 quoted below) or ordain a man as deacon or priest. The bishops take the place of the Apostles, deriving their authority from Christ's commission to the Apostles, handed down to them today. This is called the Apostolic Succession. Bishops have oversight of dioceses. These may have as few as a dozen parishes, but in some countries have as many as four or five hundred. Titles vary from country to country, but the bishop of a large diocese may have a suffragan or assistant bishop(s) and also be aided by archdeacons and rural deans who supervise groups of parishes. The dean is the chief minister of the cathedral, but if the cathedral has a parish the title provost is used.

A group of dioceses forms a province under an Archbishop, who may be referred to as the Metropolitan. In Scotland the title Archbishop is avoided and the bishop elected head of the province is called the Primus, meaning 'first among equals'. Where a country has several provinces (e.g. Canada) one of the Archbishops is appointed Primate.

CONFIRMATION

Confirmation is in the Bible. It was practised by the Apostles. We read about it in the New Testament. The Church has administered it ever since.

Confirmation: In the New Testament
From Acts, Chap. 8

Philip came down to a city in Samaria and began proclaiming the Messiah to them ... When they came to believe Philip with his good news about the kingdom of God and the name of Jesus Christ, they were baptized, men and women alike ... The Apostles in Jerusalem now heard that Samaria had accepted the word of God. They sent off Peter and John, who went down there and prayed for the converts, asking that they might receive the Holy Spirit ... So Peter and John laid their hands on them and they received the Holy Spirit.

Confirmation: Receiving the Holy Spirit

Philip had gone to Samaria preaching and teaching. He baptized his converts, just as your priest would. Then the Apostles came from Jerusalem and 'laid their hands on them and they received the Holy Spirit', i.e., confirmed them. In the same way, after you have been carefully instructed and prepared, the Bishop comes and 'lays his hands' upon you, and *you receive the Holy Spirit*. The word 'confirmation', a convenient name for this, came later. The word means 'strengthening'.

Confirmation: The Promises

At your Baptism (if in infancy) godparents made promises on your behalf. At Confirmation you make these promises yourself. You shoulder the responsibility because you are now a responsible person. But it is one thing to make a promise—it is quite another to keep that promise. You need special help, God's help. The Church calls it 'grace', strength greater than your own, power from the Holy Spirit. That power is given you at Confirmation, the laying on of hands being the outward visible sign. But it is neither automatic nor magic. You must call on that power and use it. It's rather like a cheque—little good to you till you cash it. Just having it in your pocket won't keep you from hunger.

When you are conFIRMed you make firm those promises, and are made firm to keep them by the grace and strength given you.

Confirmation: Strength for Living

Think of Confirmation as your special ordination or equipping with strength by God for your life's work. As the Sovereign when anointed at coronation is given grace to rule, or a bishop at his consecration is given grace for his high office, so you at Confirmation are given grace for your life's work, which is to fight under Christ's banner against sin, the world and the Devil and to continue Christ's faithful soldier and servant unto your life's end.

Confirmation: A Beginning

In this way Confirmation continues the process begun at Baptism. But it must not end it. That strength of the Holy Spirit given at Confirmation must be fed regularly all through your life by the Holy Communion.

THE DUTIES OF A CHURCHMAN

A Christian must live a life of discipline. Certain things are *duties*—a word not liked nowadays. They must be done always—whether we feel in the mood or not. It is by drilling ourselves to do these things that the strength of character necessary for resisting temptation is won. But we cannot do this alone in our own strength. We can do it only with God's help. The secret is to remember our Lord's presence, the power of his Holy Spirit, 'the One who stands by to help'. This power has been given to us and we must learn to call on and trust him whose strength is sufficient for us. Because a Christian knows he is never alone and practises the presence of Christ, he will be a happy, cheerful person, never downcast for long. He will be kind in his remarks and judgments about other people, always looking for the best in others. In Jesus' company (and we are in his company) we should be ashamed to say or think a mean thing, nor should we grumble or be gloomy.

So the duties of a Churchman, which help us to know Christ's presence, lead us to inward peace, quietness, and joy. We shall have the royalty of inward happiness.

These are the duties of a Churchman:

DUTY TO GOD

Worship

This is the foundation on which all else is built. By Jesus' own example in attending his place of worship, the synagogue, week by week, and also because we are told plainly in the Bible, we know that worship is the first duty of a Christian.

'Worship' means 'making God of most worth'.

The Holy Communion is the most important act of the Church's worship. Every Churchman should put it first in obedience to our Lord's command, 'DO THIS in remembrance of me'.

Prayer

Our Lord often rose a great while before the day to have enough time in his busy life for prayer. A Christian should always begin the day with prayer, and be in touch with his Heavenly Father again before he goes to bed at night. He will practise the presence of Christ, that is, remember that our Lord is with him all the time; and he will often send little 'arrow prayers'—messages of thanks, or love, or calls for help—winging their way to him.

Bible Reading

Daily reading of the Bible is far more important to a Christian than reading the daily papers. The Bible is the Christian's daily good news. It is one of the vital links between God and man. Read carefully about this on page 37.

Self-discipline

'The good which I want to do, I fail to do; but what I do is the wrong which is against my will,' said St Paul. Even he had a fight to rule himself. 'Every athlete goes into strict training. They do it to win a fading wreath; we, a wreath that never fades. For my part, I run with a clear goal before me; I am like a boxer who does not beat the air; I bruise my own body and make it know its master.'

Mastery over self is won only by constant self-discipline, and the greatest help to this is the keeping of our rule of life; that is, the rules we make for ourselves about our prayers, worship, Communion, reading of the Bible, etc.

'Fasting' is a useful aid towards this self-discipline. It means self-control in our eating, learning to deny ourselves certain foods. For example, it has for long been a custom of the Church to abstain from eating meat on Friday, the day of our Lord's Crucifixion, and on the main fast days of the Christian Year, that we may be reminded of his sacrifice for us. *He* did so much for us. We can surely do a little thing like that in acknowledgement.

Almsgiving

None of our possessions are *really* ours. God allows us the use of them. We are only stewards. This is particularly true of our money. We must put it to the best and most unselfish use.

(a) We must decide how much we ought to give to the upkeep of our Church. A regular payment system like the stewardship envelope is much better than the haphazard coin in the plate. But supporting our Church is not *giving*. It is only *paying* for what we need, just as we pay for food or clothing. It is a debt of honour, because no bill is sent.

(b) Mission is a direct command of Jesus: 'Go ye, teach all nations and baptize them'. Many can obey only by giving and by prayer.

(c) Good causes make a claim on Christian generosity. Fighting hunger and disease in many lands; care of the aged, sick or homeless; helping young and old through clubs, etc., etc.

DUTY TO OUR NEIGHBOUR

Service

We are stewards not only of our money but also of our abilities and of our time. These must be used, not only for our own enjoyment, but for the good of others. So a Christian seeks ways in which to serve. The method matters little so long as we are giving of ourselves for the benefit of others. One may teach in a Sunday school, another may run a Guide company, a third may sit at home to release a parent to get out for a little relaxation. We give invaluable service by being dependable and regular in any organization to which we belong. There are also civic and social duties, vital fields of service, neglect of which has weakened the Church.

These duties are summed up in this

Short Guide to the
Duties of Church Membership

Authorized by the
Archbishops of Canterbury and York

All baptized and confirmed members of the Church must play their full part in its life and witness. That you may fulfil this duty we call upon you:

To follow the example of Christ in home and daily life, and to bear personal witness to him.

To be regular in private prayer day by day.

To read the Bible carefully.

To come to church every Sunday.

To receive the Holy Communion faithfully and regularly.

To give personal service to Church, neighbours and community.

To give money for the work of the parish and diocese and for the work of the Church at home and overseas.

To uphold the standard of marriage entrusted by Christ to his Church.

To care that children are brought up to love and serve the Lord.

THE CHURCH'S BOOKS

I. THE BIBLE

'The most valuable thing this world affords' is how the Archbishop of Canterbury describes the Bible when, at the coronation of our Sovereigns in Westminster Abbey, he hands the Holy Scriptures to the Monarch. Yet an American journalist could give the title *The Book Nobody Knows* to a book he wrote about the Bible. The most valuable thing this world affords—the book nobody knows. Can this be so? Certainly few today know it as well as earlier generations and the whole nation is thereby poorer.

Why Is the Bible so Valuable?

(1) Because it is the record, divinely inspired, of God's dealings with mankind. The Old Testament traces the ways in which God revealed his nature to men and women, and tried to make them understand his laws, what he required from them, and his love for rich and poor alike.

The Old Testament shows how the way was prepared over the centuries for the coming into the world of Jesus Christ.

The New Testament contains four lives of Jesus (the Gospels), or more correctly, accounts of his ministry; a history of the earliest days of the Church (the Acts of the Apostles); and letters from the Apostles to congregations they had established, or to men and women who had been their friends in this work (the Epistles).

(2) Because the study of the Bible—the reading of a passage, imagining it all, and then thinking over

37

carefully what it means for us today—is one of God's appointed ways of speaking in our hearts, and making his will known.

Why 'The Book Nobody Knows'?

The Bible is not simply a book, but rather a library, for there are sixty-six books (not counting the section called the Apocrypha). The oldest books in the Old Testament were written seven or eight hundred years B.C. (before the birth of Christ); the New Testament all in the first century A.D. (Anno Domini, in the year of our Lord, i.e., since the Birth of Christ). People so long ago had different ways of thought and fashions of speech. They would have been as puzzled by our ways as we today find theirs difficult and misleading.

Then, too, the books of the Bible have been translated out of their original Hebrew or other ancient tongues.

The translation once used in all churches, the 'Authorized Version', was made over 300 years ago at the command of James I. But words develop rather different meanings over such a long period. Clearly we need all the help we can get if we are to have the greatest benefit from this 'most valuable thing the world affords'.

Nowadays most churches use new translations in up-to-date English, such as the New English Bible, the Jerusalem Bible, the Revised Standard Version, the Good News Bible or the New International Version. You should have one of these for your own use too; they are available in a wide variety of editions ranging from the very expensive to the cheap paperback.

How to Read the Bible

How much of the Bible you read is not nearly so important as *how you read it*. Offer a prayer first that God may speak to you through the passage chosen. Then read very slowly, making a great effort of imagination. Picture the scene, 'get inside' what you are reading, feel yourself there and taking part. Try to apply it to yourself. What is the message for you? Probably you will want to say a prayer about it.

All this is an art—it needs practice. Don't be disappointed if you do not get on too well at first. Persevere.

Join the Bible Reading Fellowship

To help you read your Bible regularly, the Bible Reading Fellowship publish a number of quarterly booklets. 'Awake to the Word' and 'Brief Notes' give a short explanation of the passage set and a suggestion of how it applies to your own life. 'Compass' and 'Discovery', for children and young people, each week give stories and ideas of things to do to help your Bible reading come to life. Ask your priest about it. He will strongly approve. The address of the B.R.F. is St Michael's House, 2 Elizabeth Street, London SW1W 9RQ.

II. THE PRAYER BOOK AND THE ALTERNATIVE SERVICE BOOK 1980

Before the Reformation, all church services were in Latin and contained in a number of different books. So, after the break with Rome, Archbishop Cranmer decided that all churches throughout the land should follow the same service and use just one book. He rewrote the old services in the common language so that more people could understand them, and altered them so that they were closer to what he believed the worship of the early Church had been.

Cranmer's book, the Book of Common Prayer, was taken by English people throughout the world and forms the basis for all the different prayer books used by the Churches of the worldwide Anglican Communion.

In England, however, the Prayer Book was last revised as long ago as 1662, and has never been replaced; but in 1980 a new book called The Alternative Service Book 1980 was published. This contains most of the services to be found in the Prayer Book but rewritten—just as Cranmer did in the sixteenth century—in modern English and in the light of our further knowledge about the services of the early Church. The balance between the old and the new, which the Church of England has traditionally sought to maintain, is now expressed by the use of two alternative books—the Prayer Book and the ASB.

The monks had seven 'Hours' of prayer—services or 'offices' said or sung every day. Out of these Cranmer constructed Mattins and Evensong, two services of psalms, readings and prayers, to be the daily prayer of the Church. The ASB contains shorter forms of both

Morning and Evening Prayer, which are ideal for use at home, as well as longer versions in modern English for use in church.

The Holy Communion (or the Eucharist) is everywhere the heart of the Church's worship, and probably the service you know best. In the ASB there are two versions, one in modern English (Rite A) and one in more traditional language (Rite B).

You will also find there the special prayers, 'collects', and readings from the Old and New Testaments and the Gospels for every Sunday and Holy Day of the Christian Year. When you cannot be at church on a Holy Day make a practice of reading at home the collect and readings appointed.

Both the Prayer Book and the ASB contain other great offices: Baptism, when we enter the Church, and Confirmation, when we are strengthened for our life's work; the Marriage service, when God gives men and women grace to live in a special union which should be holy; the Funeral service, when the Church lays to rest the bodies of those who have died.

The Ordinal contains the forms of service when men are ordained for the Ministry, as deacons, priests or bishops.

The Prayer Book and many editions of the ASB also contain the Psalms, the hymn-book of the Jews, which Jesus often quoted and must have known by heart.

THE CHURCH'S YEAR

The Church Calendar begins with five 'Sundays before Christmas' leading up to

ADVENT SUNDAY

(either the last Sunday in November or the first in December).

There are four Sundays in Advent and during this period the Church prepares for

CHRISTMAS

the celebration of the Birthday or First Coming of Jesus when he was born at Bethlehem, and the Son of God became man.

EPIPHANY

commemorates the revealing ('showing forth' is the exact meaning of the word) of the Divine Nature, first to the Wise Men from the East. It is observed on 6 January. There are one to six Sundays after Epiphany. Then three 'Sundays before Easter' give warning of

ASH WEDNESDAY

(preceded by Shrove Tuesday, when people confessed their sins), which is the first day of

LENT

This solemn period of discipline, repentance and growth lasts roughly forty days, the period of our Lord's special preparation in the wilderness for the opening of his Ministry. The fourth Sunday in Lent is often kept as Mothering Sunday. The fifth Sunday in Lent is called Passion Sunday. Next comes Palm Sunday, when Jesus entered into Jerusalem for the final week of teaching in the Temple, known as

HOLY WEEK

which led up to the Last Supper, on Maundy Thursday evening, immediately before he went to the Garden of Gethsemane. There he was betrayed, and taken away for trial before the High Priest in the early morning and afterwards condemned by Pontius Pilate, the Roman Governor. He was crucified later that day, called

GOOD FRIDAY

He rose from the grave on the first day of the week,

EASTER DAY

and of this event every Sunday is the commemoration week by week.

There follow the great Forty Days, when Christ appeared frequently to the disciples and others, teaching and preparing them. He withdrew his bodily presence on

ASCENSION DAY

which, being the fortieth day after Easter, always falls on a Thursday. As Christ had promised, after ten days of waiting and prayer in the Upper Room in Jerusalem, the disciples received the Holy Spirit on

WHITSUNDAY OR PENTECOST

The Holy Spirit was to lead them into all truth and strengthen them for the colossal task of making Christ known to the uttermost parts of the earth, to all men, everywhere, in all ages. Whitsunday is often known as the Birthday of the Church. As the day of the original bestowing of the Holy Spirit, it was a favourite day for Baptism. A week later, on

TRINITY SUNDAY

the Church acknowledges the glory of the Eternal Trinity, Father, Son and Holy Spirit; and for the remaining twenty or so Sundays of the year, considers the great teachings and lessons of the faith once delivered. In these the Holy Spirit is ever leading us to perceive new depths of meaning, new relevancy for the changes and chances of the passing years and the developing social scene.

At the beginning of the Prayer Book is a Calendar showing the dates when the Church honours her heroes. The Apostles are each commemorated and also some of the greatest of the Saints, and all are remembered together on All Saints' Day. The Blessed Virgin Mary is honoured on several days, especially on 8 September, and with her Son at Candlemas (2 February) and the Annunciation or Lady Day (25 March).

On Michaelmas Day the Church reverences those higher ranks of God's creation, the Holy Angels.

THE CHURCH'S COLOURS

Each type of Festival and Fast has its distinctive colour—shown in the altar frontal, vestments, stole, pulpit fall and book markers. The colours thus announce the Church's Year.

These are the main colours and their meaning:

WHITE (or cream or gold): The joyful Festivals, especially Christmas, Easter and Ascension. Also for saints other than martyrs.

RED is the colour of fire and blood, so is used for Whitsunday and for martyrs.

VIOLET (or purple) speaks of penitence and preparation—so is used in Lent and Advent.

GREEN, the ordinary colour of nature, suggests God's provision for our needs—so green is for ordinary, non-festival Sundays.

THE CHURCH'S CLOTHES:
THE VESTMENTS

Distinctive dress for various functions is worn in many callings. Not many have as long a history as church vestments, which are adaptations of the classical costumes of the Roman Empire. As styles went out of fashion for everyday wear they were retained in church use, and with modification have come down to us today. In the illustrations you will see the main vestments, and below is a list of their names and uses.

ALB—long white linen garment reaching to the ankles, derived from ancient tunic.

AMICE—once a neckcloth, has now become a linen square worn round the neck to protect the other vestments. Often decorated with an apparel.

APPARELS—ornamental panels at the foot of the alb, front and back, and on amice.

CASSOCK—the long black gown worn under other vestments. It used to be the day-to-day working costume of the clergy, not merely used in church. Some are again wearing it for day-to-day use. A bishop's cassock is purple, symbolic of rank.

CHASUBLE—worn by priest or bishop when celebrating the Holy Communion. It is descended from the commonest outdoor garment of classical times.

CHIMERE—of black or scarlet, open in front, worn by bishops over the rochet.

COPE—in the pre-Christian era it was a long cloak. It has become a costly embroidered vestment worn by bishops on occasions such as Confirmations or Ordinations, and by priests in Processions on Festivals, etc.

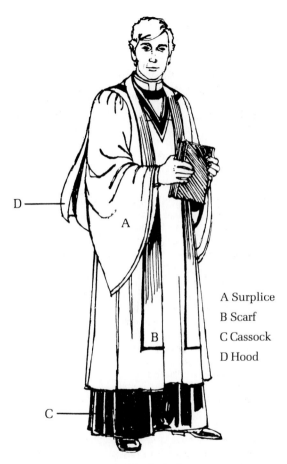

D

A

B

A Surplice
B Scarf
C Cassock
D Hood

C

Priest in choir dress

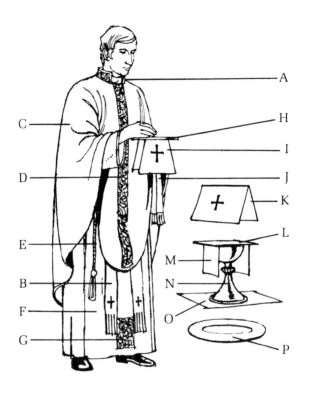

A Amice	E Girdle	I Veil	M Purificator
B Stole	F Alb	J Maniple	N Chalice
C Chasuble	G Apparel	K Burse	O Corporal
D Orphrey	H Burse	L Pall	P Paten

Priest in Eucharistic vestments

A Hood

B Chimere

C Scarf   D Rochet   E Cassock

Bishop in rochet and chimere

A Mitre

B Episcopal ring

C Pectoral cross

D Stole

E Girdle

F Alb

G Cope

H Apparel

I Crozier or pastoral staff

Bishop in cope and mitre

COTTA—similar to surplice, but shorter, especially in the sleeves. Sometimes used by clergy and servers in place of surplice.

GIRDLE—a cord used to secure the alb or cassock round the waist.

HOOD—worn by clergy at choir offices (Mattins and Evensong, etc.). Was a medieval head-dress, as name implies, but now worn hanging down the back. It denotes a university degree. Each has its distinctive colour.

MANIPLE—originally a napkin. It is worn over the left arm by bishops, priests and deacons at the Eucharist. It probably came into church use to cleanse the vessels after the stole had developed as described below.

MITRE—the head-dress of a bishop. Mitres are tongue-shaped and remind us of the tongues of fire which lighted on the Apostles at Pentecost.

ORPHREYS—the embroidered strips, usually cross-shaped, on a chasuble.

ROCHET—worn by bishops. It is like an alb, but is used without girdle or apparels.

STOLE—was once a napkin or towel carried by servants on the left shoulder. It became folded and narrow. As the deacons' duty was to cleanse the sacred vessels they wear it over the left shoulder. Priests wear the stole over both shoulders. The stole is worn at all the Sacraments.

SURPLICE—of white linen, reaching to the knees. Is worn by choir and servers as well as clergy.

TIPPET—the black scarf worn with the hood at the choir offices, etc.

PART III:
THE HOLY COMMUNION

WHAT IS
THE HOLY COMMUNION?

On the night Jesus was betrayed to his enemies and taken to be crucified, at the last supper with his friends in that upper room in Jerusalem, he gave thanks and broke bread which he blessed and they all shared, and he said: 'This is my body which is given for you. Do this in remembrance of me.' And he blessed wine and said: 'Drink ye all of this; for this is my blood of the new covenant, which is shed for you and for many for the remission of sins: do this, as oft as ye shall drink it, in remembrance of me.'

The Jews were used to a ceremonial meal as part of their worship of God, and Jesus at the Last Supper gave his friends a direct command which they could appreciate and obey. From that day to this the Sacrament of the Lord's Supper has been the central act of worship of the Church. It is known by at least six names: The Lord's Supper, The Holy Communion, The Holy Eucharist, The Blessed Sacrament (of the Body and Blood of Christ), The Mass, The Liturgy.

The Holy Communion is a Sacrament, the 'outward and visible sign of an inward and spiritual grace given unto us', in this way. The outward and visible sign is the Bread and Wine, blessed with the very words Jesus himself spoke in the upper room. The inward and spiritual grace given us is the divine life of Christ himself, grace, a share in the very nature of God. We are united with Christ, and his Spirit and Nature flow into us.

There are two parts of the Holy Communion: what man does; what God does.

What Man Does

The Holy Communion is a sacrifice, that is, a gift which people offer to God through their appointed priest, as a sign of their dependence on God, and in acknowledgement of God's absolute power and authority over them. 'Through him (Jesus Christ) we offer thee our souls and bodies to be a living sacrifice.'

But we dare not offer anything so marred and sinful as we are except through Jesus Christ; that is, by joining our unworthy offering to his perfect offering of himself, spotless and sinless.

What God Does

God accepts the offering of our sinful and unworthy selves because we unite our self-offering with the perfect offering of Jesus on Calvary. He gives to us through the Bread and Wine the divine life of Jesus, his 'grace and heavenly blessing'. He assures us of our membership with all the rest of the Church, both that part of it kneeling with us at those altar rails and other parts everywhere throughout the earth, as well as those departed from this world and now in the life beyond.

In the Holy Communion, everything in human life—our work, our homes, our love, our pleasure, leisure, hopes, fears, griefs, joys, our studies, ideas, successes, our sacrifices—all can be offered to God through Christ. All are represented in the Bread and Wine. God takes them up and consecrates them and gives them back together with the gift of divine life, so that in these things of daily life we can glorify and serve him.

Here is how a modern Prayer Book Catechism (the Canadian) puts it:

Question Why was the Sacrament of the Lord's Supper ordained?

Answer For the continual remembrance of the sacrifice of the death of Christ, and of the benefits which we receive thereby.

Question What is the outward part or sign of the Lord's Supper?

Answer Bread and Wine, which the Lord hath commanded to be received.

Question What is the inward part, or thing signified?

Answer The Body and Blood of Christ, which are verily and indeed taken and received by the faithful in the Lord's Supper.

Question What benefits do we receive thereby?

Answer The strengthening and refreshing of our souls and bodies unto eternal life by the Body and Blood of Christ.

All this is a mystery none can fully understand. It is enough that Jesus commanded us, 'Do this in remembrance of me.' To that command Christ's followers will always be faithful. If we come to Communion carefully prepared, although we shall not at first perceive all that is contained in that wonderful Sacrament—no one does—we shall find it a great source of strength, comfort and happiness.

We shall come at first because we know it is our duty and we rejoice to obey. It will not be very long before we come because we have learnt to find Jesus there, nearer than at any other time, and nothing will then keep us away from being in his Presence.

HOW OFTEN SHALL I MAKE
MY COMMUNION?

You must decide this for yourself. Be sure of two points:

(1) **Have a rule** about how often you go, and keep it.

(2) **Always prepare** thoroughly before making your Communion.

Whether you decide that it shall be every Sunday (which should be your ultimate aim), or whether you decide at first to receive the Blessed Sacrament fortnightly or monthly, is a matter you should discuss with your priest.

There are in addition 'Days of Obligation' when every communicant should be present:

Easter Day; Christmas Day; Whitsunday; Ascension Day.

Make a special point of attending on Ash Wednesday, the first day of Lent; and Maundy Thursday, the day of the Last Supper and therefore the anniversary of the institution of Holy Communion.

Come on special weekdays, too, if you can, such as Feasts of the Apostles, Lady Day, Michaelmas Day, All Saints' Day, your own birthday or other special anniversary, e.g., the anniversary of your wedding, Confirmation, or the birthday or day of the death of ones whom you love.

Would a regular weekday morning before going to work be possible? Bring to our Lord your cares and worries and also your thanksgivings and praise.

Remember: you do not need to receive Holy Communion *every* time you come.

OUR PREPARATION FOR HOLY COMMUNION

The essential things are

TO KNOW PRECISELY

what you are going to

GIVE THANKS FOR

CONFESS

PRAY FOR

Vagueness is the curse of religion. The road to hell is paved with good intentions, the things we vaguely meant to do—but of course didn't. So be very definite and clear-cut.

Think out the night before your Communion, or earlier, just exactly what you will thank God for, what you must confess, the subject for which chiefly you will pray, pleading with God for this special and particular thing, or person, the sacrifice of Jesus on the Cross. This chief subject of our praying is known as our SPECIAL INTENTION.

Go to Holy Communion so prepared that, were anyone suddenly to ask you as you entered the doors of the church, 'What are you going to THANK God for this morning?' without a moment's hesitation you could answer. In the same way, supposing you were suddenly asked 'What are you going to CONFESS to God this morning?' you could reply instantly. Or, again, if you were asked 'What is your INTENTION this morning?—that is to say, 'For what, or for whom, are you going to PRAY chiefly?'—at once you could give a definite answer.

That is the essence of a good preparation.

St Paul said:

'Anyone who eats the bread or drinks the cup of the Lord unworthily will be guilty of desecrating the body and blood of the Lord. A man must test himself before eating his share of the bread and drinking from the cup.'

DURING THE EUCHARIST

Because the Eucharist is not something done by the priest alone for the congregation but offered in Christ's name by all the people, it is important for each person to join fully in the celebration. Do this by following the service attentively, joining in the prayers said by all and saying 'Amen' or the appropriate response to the prayers led by the priest or one of the congregation. In this way you can make all the prayers your own.

Before the Service Begins

People usually kneel to pray before the Holy Communion service starts. Go over in your mind your preparation. Lay out ready, as it were, those things you decided to *thank* God for, to *confess*, and to *pray* for. Consider each carefully. Offer each to our Lord. Pray about them. Pray for the priest and all your fellow communicants in the church.

The Word and the Prayers

After the greeting and opening prayers, including the Collect, the prayer which 'collects' all our prayers for the day together, listen carefully to the Readings and reflect on them; some churches observe a helpful silence after each reading. Every Sunday there should be a sermon; this will help us understand the Readings more fully and enable us to proclaim the Gospel with more confidence in our daily lives.

The Prayers of Intercession give us the opportunity to pray for all who need our prayers—the Church, the world, the local community, the sick and those in need, and the dead. Then the priest invites us to join in the Prayers of Penitence. Before saying the Confession and receiving God's forgiveness, briefly call to mind your sins and your desire to do better.

The Ministry of the Sacrament

After we have shown our fellowship with one another at the Peace, the Bread and Wine are placed on the altar. The Bread and Wine are things people have made. They represent our work, our whole life, and they are offered to God. At this point offer your whole work, all you do all day long, to God. Then *thank* him. The money you put in the plate is your acknowledgement that all you have depends on him. 'All things come of thee, O Lord, and of thine own do we give thee.' Offer him your thanksgivings for all you have and are.

After the Prayer of Consecration, Christ is present, in the consecrated Bread and Wine. Before you receive Communion, *adore* him. Try to realize that he is there with you in the church, his house. Though unseen and invisible he is just as truly present. You cannot see the air, but you breathe it. This Communion is a meeting-place with your Lord.

Thee we adore, O hidden Saviour, thee,
Who in thy Sacrament dost deign to be;
Both Flesh and Spirit at thy Presence fail,
Yet here thy Presence we devoutly hail.

Pour out your love, your worship. Now is the time to pray about your special intention, the people or

matters you made ready at your preparation for this moment.

You go and kneel at the altar rails. Worship and adore your Saviour. Bring him again all that you decided in your preparation—your thanksgivings, confession, and special intercessions.

After the Communion

After you have received Communion, give thanks for the wonderful thing that has happened to you, for the precious gift of grace you have been given—that you have been with our Lord. From your confession there will likely arise a good resolution, e.g. if you have neglected your prayers, you must resolve most firmly to overcome this sin, and become faithful and regular in your praying. Make your resolution quite definite. It is the best possible way to thank our Lord.

Here is a summary:

Before the service begins: Go over your preparation. Lay out ready what you will thank God for, confess, pray for. Pray for the priest and the congregation.

At the Prayers of Penitence: Recall your sins and your sorrow for them.

At the Preparation of the Bread and Wine: Give thanks and offer your daily life and work.

At the Communion: Worship Christ present in the Sacrament. Pray for your special intention.

After Communion: Give thanks for your Communion and make a good resolution.

Use this method Sunday by Sunday until it is your habit. It will help greatly.

PART IV:
THE FORGIVENESS OF SINS

HOW WE ARE FORGIVEN

Can you remember as a child getting into some scrape, and before you were forgiven having to go and tell your father you were sorry? It is the same in our religion. Before God forgives us our sins we must tell him we are sorry—we have to confess our sins. There are several things involved in this. First we must be truly sorry about our sins (and remember, the good we have failed to do, the prayers we have failed to offer, rank as sin just as much as the wrong or evil we have said or thought or done). It is more a matter of the *will* than of feelings, purposing with all the strength of character that we have to improve—to do the good we have previously failed to do, to avoid the evil. But we must ask and use God's help, because we cannot do it in your own strength. Having that intention we tell God how we have failed. He knows already, of course, but like every father he wants us to own up, and *face* up. Jesus taught us that then, when we have done this, God removes the guilt. We are forgiven.

There are two ways of confessing our sins. Both bring forgiveness when we really repent, really intend to do better.

The first way is privately—it may be either kneeling by our own bedside or it may be in church—telling God in our own words in secret what our sins have been, how firmly we mean to do better, and begging for forgiveness. When that is sincere God forgives. There is no doubt of that. We have Jesus' promise.

There are words to help in this in Evening Prayers on page 12.

The second way to confess our sins to God is in the presence of some 'discreet and learned minister of God's Word', who will give us advice and help 'to the quietening of our conscience and the avoidance of all scruple and doubtfulness', and then, acting as God's spokesman, assure us of God's forgiveness.

For more about this second way, see page 68.

Before using either we need to try to see ourselves as we must appear in God's sight. We take a rosy view of ourselves, and excuse ourselves too easily. We should, therefore, in self-examination, prod memory and conscience by questions designed to let us see ourselves more as God sees us and as we really are.

See below: Overhauling Ourselves; and page 64, Questions for Self-examination.

OVERHAULING OURSELVES

Each evening in our prayers we review what we have done or left undone in the day now past, and ask forgiveness for the sins revealed.

Before each Communion (be it weekly, fortnightly, or monthly, or on special Holy Days of the Church, or on our birthday), we require to examine ourselves more strictly—else we shall not know precisely what we must confess. And unless we know what we are asking forgiveness for, how can we expect God to forgive us? For we must come cleansed and forgiven to our Communion. This forgiveness is the 'wedding garment' Christ told us we must wear at the King's banquet. So questions for self-examination are provided on pages 65 to 67, and the instruction on Forgiveness, page 62.

Just as houses require spring-cleaning, so we need 'spring-cleaning', at least once a year, or probably more often. Before our Communion at the great Festivals, especially Easter and Christmas, is the best time for an extra special overhaul, to see whether we are advancing or falling back in our fight to become people on whom Christ can rely.

For this, use with care the questions which follow, especially if you have decided to seek 'comfort and counsel' from some 'discreet and learned minister of God's Word', as the Prayer Book puts it, in order to receive the 'benefit of absolution'.

Many who are trying hard to advance in service of our Lord and his Church have decided to do this if only for the spiritual counsel and advice received.

QUESTIONS FOR
SELF-EXAMINATION

A good plan is to have paper and pencil and jot down the things we must confess. Just write single words, e.g. 'lying', jealousy', 'prayers missed'. You can put this paper in your prayer book and use it after you arrive in church in the minutes before the service begins, praying about these sins and asking for strength to overcome them. Having a paper ensures that you remember everything.

Kneel down. Think of our Lord on the Cross. Remember it was the wickedness and unlovingness of ordinary people like us which caused his death. Say a prayer such as this:

Holy Spirit, help me now to know the truth about myself. Stir up my conscience and memory that I may perceive how I have failed. Show me my sins against God and my sins against my fellows, the evil I have done and the good I have not done, so that I may truly repent and determine to do better and overcome my faults, with your help; for Jesus' sake.

The Things Left Undone

(Sins of Omission)

Have I omitted my morning prayers?—my evening prayers?—been careless in them?

Have I kept Sunday holy?

Have I stayed away from the Holy Communion on Sunday when I could have been there?

Have I prepared carefully before receiving Holy Communion?

Have I kept my rule about Bible reading?

Have I done what I ought and could—for the Church?—in my home?—for others?

Have I let slide a chance to do a kind act?—or say a kind word?—or stand up for my Faith?

Have I given as much money as I could afford for the work of the Church at home and overseas?

Have I really tried constantly to make God of most worth in my life?—or let dancing, the cinema, television, or lying in bed interfere with my duty to him?

The Things We Ought Not to Have Done

(Sins of Commission)

In Thought

Have I thought uncharitably about others?—been jealous?

Have I been conceited?—vain?—cocksure?—contemptuous?

Have I harboured malice or hatred in my heart?

Have I been spiteful?—unforgiving?

Have I let linger in my mind impure thoughts or imaginings, or desires?

In Word

Have I made fun of holy things?—spoken irreverently?—used God's name lightly?

Have I used bad language?—told dirty jokes?

Have I been strictly truthful?

Have I gossiped?—slandered others?—spoken unkindly about others?—boasted?

In Deed

Have I done my best at my work?

Have I stolen?—cheated?—delayed to pay my debts?—broken my word?

Have I been bad-tempered?—grumbled?—quarrelled?

Have I been greedy?—eaten or drunk more than my share or more than I needed?

Have I treated women and girls honourably, chivalrously and politely?—or tried to be smart?—to show off?

Have I made boys respect me?—or have I lowered the dignity of womanhood?

Have I been pure and clean and healthy in all that I do alone?—with others?

Have I taught evil to another?—set a bad example?—at home?—at work?—with my friends?

CONFESSION

To reach even a low standard of Christian living means a hard struggle. We are conscious of besetting sins which get the better of us constantly. We long for help in overcoming them. We know that our Lord is calling us not to a minimum standard but to holiness. How are we to attain it? Sometimes, too, old sins worry us. We do not feel 'right' with God.

The Prayer Book puts it this way: 'If there be any of you who by this means (i.e., private confession) cannot quiet his own conscience herein, but requireth further comfort or counsel, let him come to me or to some other discreet and learned minister of God's Word, and open his grief; that by the ministry of God's Holy Word he may receive the benefit of absolution, together with spiritual counsel and advice ...'

The Church makes available to us skilled advice to help us in life's battle. Just as ailments of the body show symptoms which a doctor is trained to recognize and treat, so a priest who is a good director is trained to recognize the ailments of the soul and treat them through the 'spiritual counsel and advice' he gives.

Two good reasons, therefore, given us in the Prayer Book for seeking this help are:

(1) The counsel and advice a wise priest can give which can help so greatly.

(2) The certainty of forgiveness and the joy this brings.

Should you decide to ask your priest to advise you in this way the times when he is available are

sometimes made known in church or on the notice-
board, or you may prefer to seek him in his own house.
He will be very happy to help you. Or, if you prefer,
you may go to a priest who is a stranger—'Come to me
or to some other discreet and learned minister,' the
Prayer Book says.

When you have talked to the priest he may ask you
to kneel and use this form of words:

Priest The Lord be in thy heart and on thy lips that
thou mayest faithfully and truly confess thy sins unto
him, to the honour and glory of his holy Name.

You now say:

**I confess to God Almighty, the Father, the Son and the
Holy Ghost and before the whole company of heaven,
and to you, my father, that I have sinned exceedingly
in thought, word, and deed, through my own
grievous fault.**

Especially I have sinned in these ways ....

*(Here name all the sins you can remember. Refer to
the list you made at your self-examination.)*

**For these and all my other sins which I cannot now
remember, I am very sorry. I intend to lead a new life.
I humbly ask pardon of God, and of you, my father,
counsel and absolution.**

*The priest will give you advice. Then he will
pronounce God's forgiveness in the Prayer Book
words:*

Our Lord Jesus Christ who hath left power to his
Church to absolve all sinners who truly repent and

69

believe in him, of his great mercy forgive thee thine offences; and by his authority committed unto me, I absolve thee from all thy sins, in the name of the Father, and of the Son, and of the Holy Ghost. *Amen.*

And he may add:

The Passion of our Lord Jesus Christ and his infinite merits be to thee for remission of sins, for growth in grace, and for the reward of everlasting life.

The Blessing of God Almighty, the Father, the Son, and the Holy Ghost, be with you now and evermore. *Amen.*

Go in peace. The Lord hath put away thy sins from thee.

Thank God with all your heart for his wonderful generosity and kindness in thus forgiving you.

THE
HOLY COMMUNION
according to

RITE B
The Alternative Service Book 1980

NOTES

Sections not preceded by the symbol ▶ may be omitted.

Texts in bold type are to be said or sung by the congregation.

The numbers [ASB/179], etc., indicate the corresponding page in The Alternative Service Book 1980.

THE WORD AND THE PRAYERS

THE PREPARATION

1. *At the entry of the ministers A SENTENCE may be used;*
    and A HYMN, A CANTICLE, or A PSALM may be sung.

2. *The minister may say*

    The Lord be with you
    All   and with thy spirit.

3. *This prayer may be said.*

    All   Almighty God,
    unto whom all hearts be open,
    all desires known,
    and from whom no secrets are hid:
    cleanse the thoughts of our hearts
    by the inspiration of thy Holy Spirit,
    that we may perfectly love thee,
    and worthily magnify thy holy name;
    through Christ our Lord. Amen.

4. *One of the following may be used.*

    Either THE COMMANDMENTS (section 55);
    or THE SUMMARY OF THE LAW (section 56);
    or KYRIE ELEISON in English or Greek (section 57),
    each petition being said once, twice, or three times.

5. *GLORIA IN EXCELSIS may be said.*

All   **Glory be to God on high,**
       and in earth peace, good will towards men.

       We praise thee, we bless thee,
       we worship thee, we glorify thee,
       we give thanks to thee for thy great glory,
       O Lord God, heavenly King,
       God the Father almighty.

       O Lord, the only-begotten Son, Jesus Christ:
       O Lord God, Lamb of God, Son of the Father,
       that takest away the sins of the world,
       have mercy upon us.
       Thou that takest away the sins of the world,
       receive our prayer.
       Thou that sittest at the right hand of God
         the Father,
       have mercy upon us.

       For thou only art holy;
       thou only art the Lord;
       thou only, O Christ,
       with the Holy Ghost,
       art the Most High,
       in the glory of God the Father. Amen.

▶ 6.   *THE COLLECT*

THE MINISTRY OF THE WORD

▶ 7.   *Either two or three readings from scripture follow, the last of which is always the Gospel.*

8.   **Sit.** *OLD TESTAMENT READING. At the end the reader may say*

       This is the word of the Lord.
All   **Thanks be to God.**

9. *A PSALM may be used.*

10. **Sit.** *NEW TESTAMENT READING (EPISTLE).*
    At the end the reader may say

    This is the word of the Lord.
    All   Thanks be to God.

11. *A CANTICLE, A HYMN, or A PSALM may be used.*

▶ 12. **Stand.** *THE GOSPEL. When it is announced*

    All   Glory be to thee, O Lord.

    At the end the reader says

    This is the Gospel of Christ.
    All   Praise be to thee, O Christ.

▶ 13. **Sit.** *THE SERMON*

▶ 14. **Stand.** *THE NICENE CREED is said on Sundays and other Holy Days, and may be said on other days.*

    **All   I believe in one God
    the Father almighty,
    maker of heaven and earth,
    and of all things visible and invisible:**

    **And in one Lord Jesus Christ,
    the only-begotten Son of God,
    begotten of his Father before all worlds,
    God of God, Light of Light,
    very God of very God,
    begotten, not made,
    being of one substance with the Father,
    by whom all things were made;
    who for us men and for our salvation
    came down from heaven,
    and was incarnate by the Holy Ghost
       of the Virgin Mary,**

and was made man,
and was crucified also for us
   under Pontius Pilate.
He suffered and was buried,
and the third day he rose again
according to the scriptures,
and ascended into heaven,
and sitteth on the right hand of the Father.
And he shall come again with glory
to judge both the quick and the dead:
whose kingdom shall have no end.

And I believe in the Holy Ghost,
the Lord, the Giver of life,
who proceedeth from the Father
   and the Son,
who with the Father and the Son together
   is worshipped and glorified,
who spake by the prophets.
And I believe one holy catholic and
   apostolic Church.
I acknowledge one baptism for the
   remission of sins.
And I look for the resurrection
   of the dead,
and the life of the world to come. Amen.

PRAYERS OF INTERCESSION

15. *Banns of marriage and other notices may be published;
the offerings of the people may be collected and
presented; a hymn may be sung; and verses of scripture
may be read.*

▶ 16. INTERCESSIONS *are led by the priest, or by others.
These may be introduced by biddings. It is not necessary
to include specific subjects in any section of the
following prayers. The set passages may follow one*

another as a continuous whole, or this versicle and response may be used after each paragraph.

Minister	Lord, in thy mercy
All	**hear our prayer.**

Either section 17 or section 18 is used.

17. *FIRST INTERCESSION. The minister says*

Let us pray for the whole Church of God in Christ Jesus, and for all men according to their needs.

Almighty and everliving God, who by thy holy apostle hast taught us to make prayers and supplications, and to give thanks, for all men: we humbly beseech thee most mercifully *(to accept our alms and oblations, and) to receive these our prayers, which we offer unto thy divine majesty; beseeching thee to inspire continually the universal Church with the spirit of truth, unity, and concord; and grant that all they that do confess thy holy name may agree in the truth of thy holy word, and live in unity and godly love.

We beseech thee also to lead all nations in the way of righteousness and peace; and so to direct all kings and rulers, that under them thy people may be godly and quietly governed. And grant unto thy servant Elizabeth our Queen and to all that are put in authority under her, that they may truly and impartially administer justice, to the punishment of wickedness and vice, and to the maintenance of thy true religion and virtue. Give grace, O heavenly Father, to all bishops, priests, and deacons, especially to thy servant N our

If the offerings of the people have not been presented these words in brackets are omitted.

bishop, that they may both by their life and doctrine set forth thy true and lively word and rightly and duly administer thy holy sacraments.

Guide and prosper, we pray thee, those who are labouring for the spread of thy gospel among the nations, and enlighten with thy Spirit all places of education and learning; that the whole world may be filled with the knowledge of thy truth.

And to all thy people give thy heavenly grace; and specially to this congregation here present, that with meek heart and due reverence, they may hear and receive thy holy word; truly serving thee in holiness and righteousness all the days of their life.

And we most humbly beseech thee of thy goodness, O Lord, to comfort and succour all them who in this transitory life are in trouble, sorrow, need, sickness, or any other adversity.

And we commend to thy gracious keeping, O Lord, all thy servants departed this life in thy faith and fear, beseeching thee, according to thy promises, to grant them refreshment, light, and peace.

And here we give thee most high praise and hearty thanks for all thy saints, who have been the chosen vessels of thy grace, and lights of the world in their several generations; and we pray that, rejoicing in their fellowship and following their good examples, we may be partakers with them of thy heavenly kingdom.

Grant this, O Father, for Jesus Christ's sake, our only mediator and advocate, who liveth and reigneth with thee in the unity of the Holy Spirit, one God, world without end. **Amen.**

The service continues at either section 19 or section 20.

18. SECOND INTERCESSION

Minister Let us pray for the whole Church of God in Christ Jesus, and for all men according to their needs.

Almighty God, who hast promised to hear the prayers of those who ask in faith:

Here he may pray for the Church throughout the world, especially for the diocese and its bishop; and for any particular needs of the Church.

Grant that we and all who confess thy name may be united in thy truth, live together in thy love, and show forth thy glory in the world.

Here he may pray for the nations of the world, for this kingdom, and for all men in their various callings.

Give wisdom to all in authority, bless Elizabeth our Queen, and direct this nation and all nations in the ways of justice and of peace; that men may honour one another, and seek the common good.

Here he may pray for the local community; for families, friends, and particular persons.

Give grace to us, our families and friends, and to all our neighbours in Christ, that we may serve him in one another, and love as he loves us.

Here he may pray for the sick, the poor, and those in trouble, and for the needs of particular persons.

Save and comfort those who suffer, that they may hold to thee through good and ill, and trust in thy unfailing love.

Here he may commemorate the departed; he may commend them by name.

Hear us as we remember those who have died in faith, and grant us with them a share in thy eternal kingdom.

Merciful Father,

All   **accept these prayers,**
for the sake of thy Son,
our Saviour Jesus Christ. Amen.

PRAYERS OF PENITENCE

19. *The minister may say one or more of*
THE COMFORTABLE WORDS.

Hear what comfortable words our Saviour Christ says to all who truly turn to him: Come unto me, all that travail, and are heavy laden, and I will refresh you.   *Matthew 11.28*

So God loved the world, that he gave his only-begotten Son, to the end that all that believe in him should not perish, but have everlasting life.
John 3.16

Hear what Saint Paul says: This is a true saying and worthy of all men to be received, that Christ Jesus came into the world to save sinners.
1 Timothy 1.15

Hear what Saint John says: If any man sin, we have an advocate with the Father, Jesus Christ the righteous; and he is the propitiation for our sins.   *1 John 2.1*

▶ 20. Minister   *(Ye that do truly and earnestly repent you of your sins, and are in love and charity with your neighbours, and intend to lead a new life,

The words in brackets may be omitted.

following the commandments of God, and walking from henceforth in his holy ways;) draw near with faith, and take this holy sacrament to your comfort; and make your humble confession to almighty God (meekly kneeling upon your knees).

or Seeing we have a great high priest who has passed into the heavens, Jesus the Son of God, let us draw near with a true heart, in full assurance of faith, and make our confession to our heavenly Father.

▶ 21. **Kneel**

All   **Almighty God, our heavenly Father,**
we have sinned against thee,
through our own fault,
in thought, and word, and deed,
and in what we have left undone.
We are heartily sorry,
and repent of all our sins.
For thy Son our Lord Jesus Christ's sake,
forgive us all that is past;
and grant that we may serve thee in newness
** of life,**
to the glory of thy name. Amen.

▶ 22. Priest   Almighty God,
who forgives all who truly repent,
have mercy upon *you*,
pardon and deliver *you* from all *your* sins,
confirm and strengthen *you* in all
   goodness,
and keep *you* in life eternal;
through Jesus Christ our Lord. **Amen.**

23. *All may say*

We do not presume
to come to this thy table, O merciful Lord,
trusting in our own righteousness,
but in thy manifold and great mercies.
We are not worthy
so much as to gather up the crumbs under
    thy table.
But thou art the same Lord
whose nature is always to have mercy.
Grant us therefore, gracious Lord,
so to eat the flesh of thy dear Son
    Jesus Christ
and to drink his blood,
*(that our sinful bodies may be made clean
    by his body
and our souls washed through his most
    precious blood, and)
that we may evermore dwell in him
and he in us. Amen.

*The words in brackets may be omitted.

THE MINISTRY OF THE SACRAMENT

THE PEACE

24. **Stand**
   Priest   We are the Body of Christ.
           By one Spirit we were all baptized into one body.
           Endeavour to keep the unity of the Spirit
           in the bond of peace.

   He then says

           The peace of the Lord be always with you
   All   **and with thy spirit.**

25. *All may exchange a sign of peace.*

THE PREPARATION OF THE BREAD AND WINE

26. *The priest begins THE OFFERTORY.*
   The bread and the wine are placed on the holy table.

27. *The offerings of the people may be collected and*
   presented if this has not already been done. These words
   may be used.

   > **Thine, O Lord, is the greatness and**
   >   **the power**
   > **and the glory and the victory and**
   >   **the majesty.**
   > **All that is in heaven and earth is thine.**
   > **All things come of thee, O Lord,**
   > **and of thine own do we give thee.**

28. *At the preparation of the gifts A HYMN may be sung.*

THE THANKSGIVING

▶ 29. *The priest says THE PRAYER OF CONSECRATION using either section 30 or section 31.*

▶ 30. *FIRST THANKSGIVING*

Priest The Lord be with you
All **and with thy spirit.**

Priest Lift up your hearts.
All **We lift them up unto the Lord.**

Priest Let us give thanks unto the Lord our God.
All **It is meet and right so to do.**

Priest It is very meet, right, and our bounden duty,
that we should at all times and in all places
give thanks unto thee,
O Lord, holy Father,
almighty, everlasting God,
Creator of heaven and earth,

PROPER PREFACE, when appropriate (section 52). The following is used when no Proper Preface is provided.

· through Jesus Christ our Lord; for he is the true High Priest, who has washed us from our sins, and has made us to be a kingdom and priests unto thee, our God and Father.

Therefore with angels and archangels,
and with all the company of heaven,
we laud and magnify thy glorious name,
evermore praising thee and saying:

Holy, holy, holy, Lord God of Hosts,
heaven and earth are full of thy glory.
Glory be to thee, O Lord most high. (Amen.)

(Blessed is he that cometh in the name of
the Lord.
Hosanna in the highest.)

All glory be to thee,
almighty God, our heavenly Father,
who of thy tender mercy
didst give thine only Son Jesus Christ
to suffer death upon the cross
    for our redemption;
who made there,
by his one oblation of himself once offered,
a full, perfect, and sufficient sacrifice,
    oblation, and satisfaction
for the sins of the whole world;
and did institute,
and in his holy gospel command us to continue,
a perpetual memory of that his precious death,
until his coming again.

Hear us, O merciful Father,
we most humbly beseech thee;
and grant that by the power of thy Holy Spirit,
we receiving these thy creatures
    of bread and wine,
according to thy Son our Saviour
    Jesus Christ's holy institution,
in remembrance of his death and passion,
may be partakers
    of his most blessed body and blood.
Who, in the same night that he was betrayed,
took bread; *Here the priest is to take the
paten into his hands.*
and when he had given thanks,
he brake it, *Here he may break the bread.*
and gave it to his disciples, saying, Take, eat;
Here he is to lay his hand upon the bread.
this is my body which is given for you:
do this in remembrance of me.
Likewise after supper he took the cup;
Here he is to take the cup into his hand.
and when he had given thanks,
he gave it to them, saying, Drink ye all of this;

Here to lay his hand upon the cup.
for this is my blood of the New Testament,
which is shed for you and for many
for the remission of sins:
do this, as oft as ye shall drink it,
in remembrance of me.

Wherefore, O Lord and heavenly Father,
we thy humble servants,
having in remembrance
the precious death and passion of thy dear Son,
his mighty resurrection and glorious ascension,
entirely desire thy fatherly goodness
mercifully to accept this our sacrifice
    of praise and thanksgiving;
most humbly beseeching thee to grant that
by the merits and death of thy Son Jesus Christ,
and through faith in his blood,
we and all thy whole Church
may obtain remission of our sins,
and all other benefits of his passion.
And although we be unworthy
    through our manifold sins
to offer unto thee any sacrifice,
yet we beseech thee to accept
    this our bounden duty and service,
not weighing our merits
    but pardoning our offences.
We pray that all we who are partakers
    of this holy communion
may be fulfilled with thy grace
    and heavenly benediction.
Through Jesus Christ our Lord,
by whom, and with whom, and in whom,
in the unity of the Holy Spirit,
all honour and glory be unto thee,
O Father almighty, world without end. **Amen.**

Silence may be kept. The service continues at either section 32 or section 33 or section 34.

[ASB/192]

31. SECOND THANKSGIVING

Priest The Lord be with you
All **and with thy spirit.**

Priest Lift up your hearts.
All **We lift them up unto the Lord.**

Priest Let us give thanks unto the Lord our God.
All **It is meet and right so to do.**

Priest It is very meet, right, and our bounden duty,
that we should at all times and in all places
give thanks unto thee,
O Lord, holy Father,
almighty, everlasting God,
through Jesus Christ
thine only Son our Lord.

Because through him thou hast created
all things from the beginning,
and fashioned us men in thine own image;

through him thou didst redeem us
from the slavery of sin,
giving him to be born as man,
to die upon the cross,
and to rise again for us;

through him thou hast made us a people
for thine own possession,
exalting him to thy right hand on high,
and sending forth through him
thy holy and life-giving Spirit.

PROPER PREFACE, when appropriate (section 53)

Therefore with angels and archangels,
and with all the company of heaven,
we laud and magnify thy glorious name,
evermore praising thee and saying,

Holy, holy, holy, Lord God of hosts,
heaven and earth are full of thy glory.
Glory be to thee, O Lord most high.

(Blessed is he that cometh in the name of
   the Lord.
Hosanna in the highest.)

Hear us, O Father,
through Christ thy Son our Lord;
through him accept our sacrifice of praise;
and grant that by the power of thy Holy Spirit
these gifts of bread and wine
may be unto us his body and blood.

Who, in the same night that he was betrayed,
took bread; *Here the priest is to take the bread
into his hands.*
and when he had given thanks to thee,
he broke it,
and gave it to his disciples, saying, Take, eat;
this is my body which is given for you:
do this in remembrance of me.

Likewise after supper he took the cup;
Here he is to take the cup into his hands.
and when he had given thanks to thee,
he gave it to them saying, Drink ye all of this;
for this is my blood of the new covenant,
which is shed for you and for many
for the remission of sins:
do this, as oft as ye shall drink it,
   in remembrance of me.

Wherefore, O Lord and heavenly Father,
with this bread and this cup
we make the memorial of his saving passion,
his resurrection from the dead,
and his glorious ascension into heaven,
and we look for the coming of his kingdom.
We pray thee to accept this
   our duty and service,

and grant that we may so eat and drink
    these holy things
in the presence of thy divine majesty,
that we may be filled with thy grace
    and heavenly blessing.

Through Jesus Christ our Lord,
by whom, and with whom, and in whom,
in the unity of the Holy Spirit,
all honour and glory be unto thee,
O Father almighty,
world without end. **Amen.**

Silence may be kept.

32. *THE BENEDICTUS may follow, if it has not already been said.*

    **Blessed is he that cometh in the name of
      the Lord.
    Hosanna in the highest.**

▶ 33. *The priest and people together say THE LORD'S PRAYER either here or at section 36, or at section 44. (The text is printed at section 36.)*

THE COMMUNION

*THE BREAKING OF THE BREAD AND
THE GIVING OF THE BREAD AND CUP*

▶ 34. *The priest breaks the consecrated bread, if he has not already done so, saying*

    We break this bread
    to share in the body of Christ.

All   **Though we are many, we are one body,
        because we all share in one bread.**

35. *Either here or during the distribution this anthem may be said.*

> O Lamb of God,
> that takest away the sins of the world,
> have mercy upon us.
>
> O Lamb of God,
> that takest away the sins of the world,
> have mercy upon us.
>
> O Lamb of God,
> that takest away the sins of the world,
> grant us thy peace.

36. *The priest and people may say THE LORD'S PRAYER, if it has not already been said.*

Priest   As our Saviour has taught us, so we pray.
All   **Our Father, who art in heaven,**
hallowed be thy name;
thy kingdom come;
thy will be done;
on earth as it is in heaven.
Give us this day our daily bread.
And forgive us our trespasses,
as we forgive those who trespass
    against us.
And lead us not into temptation;
but deliver us from evil.

For thine is the kingdom, the power,
    and the glory,
for ever and ever. Amen.

▶ 37. *The priest and people receive the communion.*

The communion may be administered in one of the following ways:

[ASB 196]

38. *The minister says to each communicant*

> The body of our Lord Jesus Christ, which was given for you, preserve your body and soul unto everlasting life. Take and eat this in remembrance that Christ died for you, and feed on him in your heart by faith with thanksgiving.

> The blood of our Lord Jesus Christ, which was shed for you, preserve your body and soul unto everlasting life. Drink this in remembrance that Christ's blood was shed for you, and be thankful.

39. *or*
The priest first says to all the communicants

> Draw near and receive the body of our Lord Jesus Christ, which was given for you, and his blood, which was shed for you. Take this in remembrance that Christ died for you, and feed on him in your hearts by faith with thanksgiving.

One of the ministers then delivers the bread to each communicant, saying

> The body of Christ.

or   The body of Christ preserve your body and soul unto everlasting life.

or   The body of our Lord Jesus Christ, which was given for you, preserve your body and soul unto everlasting life.

One of the ministers then delivers the cup to each communicant, saying

> The blood of Christ.

> *or* The blood of Christ preserve your body and soul unto everlasting life.

> *or* The blood of our Lord Jesus Christ, which was shed for you, preserve your body and soul unto everlasting life.

The communicant may reply each time **Amen**, *and then receives.*

40. *During the distribution HYMNS and ANTHEMS may be sung.*

▶ 41. *If either or both of the consecrated elements are likely to prove insufficient, the priest returns to the holy table and adds more, with these words.*

> Having given thanks to thee, O Father, over the bread and the cup according to the institution of thy Son Jesus Christ, who said, Take, eat; this is my body (and/or Drink this; this is my blood) we pray that this bread/wine also may be to us his body/blood, and be received in remembrance of him.

▶ 42. *Any consecrated bread and wine which is not required for purposes of communion is consumed at the end of the distribution, or after the service.*

AFTER COMMUNION

43. *AN APPROPRIATE SENTENCE may be said and A HYMN may be sung.*

▶ 44. *The priest and people say THE LORD'S PRAYER, if it has not already been said. (The text is printed at section 36.)*

▶ 45. *Either or both of the following PRAYERS or either of those in the Appendices (section 58) are said.*

46. Priest   Almighty and everliving God, we most heartily thank thee, for that thou dost vouchsafe to feed us, who have duly received these holy mysteries, with the spiritual food of the most precious body and blood of thy Son our Saviour Jesus Christ; and dost assure us thereby of thy favour and goodness towards us; and that we are very members incorporate in the mystical body of thy Son, which is the blessed company of all faithful people, and are also heirs through hope of thy everlasting kingdom, by the merits of the most precious death and passion of thy dear Son. And we most humbly beseech thee, O heavenly Father, so to assist us with thy grace, that we may continue in that holy fellowship, and do all such good works as thou hast prepared for us to walk in; through Jesus Christ our Lord, to whom, with thee and the Holy Spirit, be all honour and glory, world without end. **Amen.**

47. **All**   **Almighty God,**
we thank thee for feeding us
with the body and blood of thy Son
     Jesus Christ our Lord.
Through him we offer thee our souls
     and bodies
to be a living sacrifice.
Send us out
in the power of thy spirit,
to live and work
to thy praise and glory. Amen.

48. *GLORIA IN EXCELSIS may be used, if it has not been used already (the text is printed at section 5); or some other suitable canticle or hymn may be sung.*

THE DISMISSAL

49. *The priest may say this or an alternative BLESSING (section 54).*

> The peace of God, which passes all understanding, keep your hearts and minds in the knowledge and love of God, and of his Son Jesus Christ our Lord; and the blessing of God almighty, the Father, the Son, and the Holy Spirit, be among you and remain with you always. **Amen.**

▶ 50. Priest   Go in peace and serve the Lord.
     All   **In the name of Christ. Amen.**

or

    Priest   Go in the peace of Christ.
    All   **Thanks be to God.**

▶ 51. *The ministers and people depart.*

APPENDICES

52. PROPER PREFACES FOR THE FIRST THANKSGIVING

Christmas, Presentation, and Annunciation
because thou didst give Jesus Christ thine only Son to be born
for our salvation: who, by the operation of the Holy Spirit,
was made true man of the substance of the Virgin Mary his
mother: and that without spot of sin, to make us clean from
all sin.

Epiphany
through Jesus Christ our Lord: who in substance of our
mortal flesh manifested forth his glory: that he might bring all
men out of darkness into his own marvellous light.

Thursday before Easter
through Jesus Christ our Lord: who having loved his own
that were in the world loved them unto the end; and on the
night he suffered, sitting at meat with his disciples, did
institute these holy mysteries; that we, redeemed by his
death and quickened by his resurrection, might be partakers
of his divine nature.

Easter
but chiefly we are bound to praise thee for the glorious
resurrection of thy Son Jesus Christ our Lord: for he is the
true Paschal Lamb which was offered for us, and has taken
away the sin of the world; who by his death has destroyed
death, and by his rising to life again has restored to us
everlasting life.

Ascension
through thy most dearly beloved Son Jesus Christ our Lord:
who after his most glorious resurrection manifestly appeared
to all his apostles; and in their sight ascended up into heaven
to prepare a place for us; that where he is, thither we might
also ascend, and reign with him in glory.

Pentecost
through Jesus Christ our Lord: who after he had ascended up far above all the heavens, and was set down at the right hand of thy majesty, did as at this time send forth upon the universal Church thy holy and life-giving Spirit: that through his glorious power the joy of the everlasting gospel might go forth into all the world; whereby we have been brought out of darkness and error into the clear light and true knowledge of thee, and of thy Son our Saviour Jesus Christ.

Trinity Sunday
who with thine only-begotten Son and the Holy Spirit art one God, one Lord in trinity of Persons and in unity of substance: for that which we believe of thy glory, O Father, the same we believe of thy Son and of the Holy Spirit, without any difference or inequality.

Transfiguration
because the divine glory of the incarnate Word shone forth upon the holy mount before the chosen witnesses of his majesty; and thine own voice from heaven proclaimed thy beloved Son.

Saints' Days
who in the righteousness of thy saints hast given us an example of godly living, and in their blessedness a glorious pledge of the hope of our calling, that, being encompassed about with so great a cloud of witnesses, we may run with patience the race that is set before us, and with them receive the crown of glory that fadeth not away.

Consecration or Dedication of a Church
who, though the heaven of heavens cannot contain thee, and thy glory is in all the world, dost deign to hallow places for thy worship, and in them dost pour forth gifts of grace upon thy faithful people.

Funerals

because through thy Son Jesus Christ our Lord, thou hast given us eternal life, and delivered us from the bondage of sin and the fear of death into the glorious liberty of the children of God.

or

because through thy Son Jesus Christ our Lord, thou hast given us the hope of a glorious resurrection, so that although death comes to us all, yet we rejoice in the promise of eternal life; for to thy faithful people life is changed, not taken away, and when our mortal flesh is laid aside, an everlasting dwelling place is made ready for us in heaven.

53. PROPER PREFACES FOR THE SECOND THANKSGIVING

Advent
And now we give thee thanks, because the day of our deliverance has dawned; and through him thou wilt make all things new, as he comes in power and triumph to judge the world.

Christmas, Presentation, and Annunciation
And now we give thee thanks, for by the operation of the Holy Spirit, he was made man of the Virgin Mary his mother; and that without spot of sin, to make us clean from all sin.

Epiphany
And now we give thee thanks, because in coming to dwell among us as man, he revealed the radiance of his glory, and brought us out of darkness into his own marvellous light.

Lent
And now we give thee thanks, because through him thou hast given us the spirit of discipline, that we may triumph over evil and grow in grace.

Passiontide

And now we give thee thanks, because for our salvation he was obedient even to death on the cross. The tree of defeat became the tree of glory: and where life was lost, there life has been restored.

Thursday before Easter

And now we give thee thanks, because having loved his own that were in the world he loved them unto the end; and on the night before he suffered, sitting at meat with his disciples, did institute these holy mysteries; that we, redeemed by his death and quickened by his resurrection, might be partakers of his divine nature.

Easter

And now we give thee thanks, for his glorious resurrection from the dead. For he is the true Paschal Lamb which was offered for us, and has taken away the sin of the world; who by his death has destroyed death, and by his rising to life again has restored to us everlasting life.

Ascension

And now we give thee thanks, because in his risen body he appeared to his disciples and in their sight was taken into heaven, to reign with thee in glory.

Pentecost

And now we give thee thanks, because by the same Spirit we are led into all truth and are given power to proclaim thy gospel to the nations and to serve thee as a royal priesthood.

Trinity Sunday

And now we give thee thanks, because thou hast revealed thy glory as the glory of thy Son and of the Holy Spirit: three persons equal in majesty, undivided in splendour, yet one Lord, one God, ever to be worshipped and adored.

[ASB/204]

Transfiguration
And now we give thee thanks, because the divine glory of the incarnate Word shone forth upon the holy mount before the chosen witnesses of his majesty; and thine own voice from heaven proclaimed thy beloved Son.

Saints' Days
And now we give thee thanks, for the glorious pledge of the hope of our calling which thou hast given us in thy saints; that following their example and strengthened by their fellowship, we may run with perseverance the race that is set before us, and with them receive the unfading crown of glory.

Dedication
And now we give thee thanks, for thy blessings on this house of prayer, where we are stirred to faithful witness, and are built up by thy Spirit into a temple made without hands, even the body of thy Son Jesus Christ.

Funerals
And now we give thee thanks, because through him thou hast given us eternal life, and delivered us from the bondage of sin and the fear of death into the glorious liberty of the children of God.

or

And now we give thee thanks, because through him thou hast given us the hope of a glorious resurrection, so that although death comes to us all, yet we rejoice in the promise of eternal life; for to thy faithful people life is changed, not taken away, and when our mortal flesh is laid aside, an everlasting dwelling place is made ready for us in heaven.

54. ALTERNATIVE BLESSINGS

Advent
Christ the Sun of righteousness shine upon you and scatter the darkness from before your path: and the blessing...

Christmas
Christ the Son of God gladden your hearts with the good news of his kingdom: and the blessing...

Lent
Christ give you grace to grow in holiness, to deny yourselves, and to take up your cross, and follow him: and the blessing...

Passiontide
Christ crucified draw you to himself, so that you find in him a sure ground for faith, a firm support for hope, and the assurance of sins forgiven: and the blessing...

Easter
The God of peace, who brought again from the dead our Lord Jesus, that great shepherd of the sheep, make you perfect in every good work to do his will: and the blessing...

Ascension
Christ our king make you faithful and strong to do his will, that you may reign with him in glory: and the blessing...

Pentecost
The Spirit of truth lead you into all truth, give you grace to confess that Jesus Christ is Lord, and to proclaim the word and works of God: and the blessing...

Trinity Sunday
God the Holy Trinity make you strong in faith and love, defend you on every side, and guide you in truth and peace: and the blessing...

Saints' Days
God give you grace to follow his saints in faith and hope and love: and the blessing...

Unity
Christ the Good Shepherd, who laid down his life for his sheep, draw you and all who hear his voice to be one within one fold: and the blessing...

[ASB/206]

Minister	God spake these words and said: I am the Lord thy God, thou shalt have none other gods but me.
All	**Lord, have mercy upon us,** **and incline our hearts to keep this law.**

Minister	Thou shalt not make to thyself any graven image, nor the likeness of anything that is in heaven above, or in the earth beneath, or in the water under the earth. Thou shalt not bow down to them, nor worship them.
All	**Lord, have mercy upon us,** **and incline our hearts to keep this law.**

Minister	Thou shalt not take the name of the Lord thy God in vain.
All	**Lord, have mercy upon us,** **and incline our hearts to keep this law.**

Minister	Remember that thou keep holy the Sabbath day. Six days shalt thou labour, and do all that thou hast to do; but the seventh day is the Sabbath of the Lord thy God.
All	**Lord, have mercy upon us,** **and incline our hearts to keep this law.**

Minister	Honour thy father and thy mother.
All	**Lord, have mercy upon us,** **and incline our hearts to keep this law.**

Minister	Thou shalt do no murder.
All	**Lord, have mercy upon us,** **and incline our hearts to keep this law.**

Minister	Thou shalt not commit adultery.
All	**Lord, have mercy upon us,** **and incline our hearts to keep this law.**

| Minister | Thou shalt not steal. |
| **All** | **Lord, have mercy upon us,**
and incline our hearts to keep this law. |

| Minister | Thou shalt not bear false witness. |
| **All** | **Lord, have mercy upon us,**
and incline our hearts to keep this law. |

| Minister | Thou shalt not covet. |
| **All** | **Lord, have mercy upon us,**
and write all these thy laws in our hearts,
we beseech thee. |

56. *THE SUMMARY OF THE LAW*

Minister   Our Lord Jesus Christ said: Hear O Israel, the Lord our God is one Lord; and thou shalt love the Lord thy God with all thy heart, and with all thy soul, and with all thy mind, and with all thy strength. This is the first commandment. And the second is like, namely this: Thou shalt love thy neighbour as thyself. There is none other commandment greater than these. On these two commandments hang all the law and

All   **Lord, have mercy upon us,**
and write all these thy laws in our hearts,
we beseech thee.

57. *KYRIE ELEISON*

Lord, have mercy (upon us.)	Kyrie eleison.
Lord, have mercy (upon us.)	**Kyrie eleison.**
Lord, have mercy (upon us.)	Kyrie eleison.

Christ, have mercy (upon us.)	**Christe eleison.**
Christ, have mercy (upon us.)	Christe eleison.
Christ, have mercy (upon us.)	**Christe eleison.**

Lord, have mercy (upon us.)	Kyrie eleison.
Lord, have mercy (upon us.)	**Kyrie eleison.**
Lord, have mercy (upon us.)	Kyrie eleison.

58. ALTERNATIVE PRAYERS

Either of the following prayers may be used instead of those in sections 46 and 47.

Priest   O Lord and heavenly Father, we thy humble servants entirely desire thy fatherly goodness mercifully to accept this our sacrifice of praise and thanksgiving; most humbly beseeching thee to grant, that by the merits and death of thy Son Jesus Christ, and through faith in his blood, we and all thy whole Church may obtain remission of our sins, and all other benefits of his passion. And here we offer and present unto thee, O Lord, ourselves, our souls and bodies, to be a reasonable, holy, and lively sacrifice unto thee; humbly beseeching thee, that all we, who are partakers of this Holy Communion, may be fulfilled with thy grace and heavenly benediction. And although we be unworthy, through our manifold sins, to offer unto thee any sacrifice, yet we beseech thee to accept this our bounden duty and service, not weighing our merits, but pardoning our offences; through Jesus Christ our Lord, by whom, and with whom, in the unity of the Holy Ghost, all honour and glory be unto thee, O Father almighty, world without end. **Amen.**

All   **Almighty Lord, and everlasting God,
we offer and present unto thee ourselves,
    our souls and bodies,
to be a reasonable, holy, and living
    sacrifice unto thee:
humbly beseeching thee,
that all we, who are partakers of this Holy
    Communion,
may be fulfilled with thy grace and heavenly
    benediction.**

And although we be unworthy, through our
    manifold sins,
to offer unto thee any sacrifice,
yet we beseech thee to accept this our bounden
    duty and service,
not weighing our merits, but pardoning our
    offences;
through Jesus Christ our Lord,
to whom, with thee and the Holy Ghost,
be all honour and glory, world without end.
Amen.

[ASB/210]

NOTES

1. *Seasonal Material* The seasonal sentences (sections 1, 43) and blessings (section 54) are optional. Any other appropriate scriptural sentences may be read at sections 1 and 43 at the discretion of the priest and 'Alleluia' may be added to any sentence from Easter Day until Pentecost (Whit Sunday).

2. *1662 Material* It is permitted to use the 1662 text of the Gloria (sections 5, 48), the Creed (section 14), the Intercession (sections 17, 18), the Confession (section 21), the Absolution (section 22), and the Lord's Prayer (sections 33, 36, 44) instead of the texts printed here.

3. *Gloria in excelsis (section 5)* This canticle is also appropriate at sections 1, 11, and 48.

4. *Collects and Readings* The collects and readings are either those set out in The Alternative Service Book 1980 or those in the Book of Common Prayer, together with any others approved by the General Synod.

5. *The Sermon* The sermon (section 13) is an integral part of the Ministry of the Word. A sermon should normally be preached at all celebrations on Sundays and other Holy Days.

6. *The Peace* The priest may accompany the words of the Peace (sections 24, 25) with a handclasp or similar action; and both the words and the action may be passed through the congregation.

7. *The Prayers of Intercession and The Thanksgiving (sections 17, 18, and 30, 31)* The use of the first Intercession does not presume the use of the first Thanksgiving. Either Prayer of Intercession may be used with either Thanksgiving.

8. *Proper Prefaces*   The Proper Prefaces set out for use in the first Thanksgiving and those for Christmas, Passiontide, Easter and Ascension in the second Thanksgiving are obligatory.

9. *The First Thanksgiving (section 30)*   The Prayer of Humble Access may, if desired, be said after the Sanctus; and the Thanksgiving may end after the words, 'Do this, as oft as ye shall drink it, in remembrance of me'; in which case the people then say **Amen.**

10. *The Blessing (section 49)*   In addition to the blessings provided here and at section 54 the priest may at his discretion use others.

11. *Notices*   Banns of marriage and other notices may be published after section 1, section 12, or section 42, if they are not published at section 15.

12. *Hymns, Canticles, The Peace, The Collection and Presentation of the Offerings of the People, and The Preparation of the Gifts of Bread and Wine*   Points are indicated for these, but if occasion requires they may occur elsewhere.

13. *Silence*   After sections 8, 10, 12, 13, 20, 43 and after the biddings in sections 17, 18 silence may be kept.

14. *A Service without Communion*   When there is no communion the minister reads the service as far as the Absolution (section 22) and then adds the Lord's Prayer (section 36), the General Thanksgiving, and/or other prayers at his discretion, ending with the Grace. When such a service is led by a deacon or lay person, 'us' is said instead of 'you' in the Absolution.

PERSONAL PRAYERS AND THANKSGIVING
AFTER HOLY COMMUNION

After receiving Communion or at the end of the service, remember to give thanks for the gift of Christ's Body and Blood and for all that God has done for us.

We thank you, Lord, that you have fed us in this sacrament, united us with Christ, and given us a foretaste of the heavenly banquet prepared for all mankind.

We thank you, heavenly Father, for all your goodness to us and to all men.

For the world in which you have placed us, with its wonder and beauty. For life and health, for food and clothing, for kind friends and happy homes. For those who love us, and for all who have shown in their lives a good example. Most of all, for Jesus Christ, your only Son our Saviour, who came into the world and died for us on the cross, and rose again from the dead, and is now our Friend in heaven.

With him, and in him, and through him, by the power of the Holy Spirit, with all who stand before you in earth and heaven, we worship you, Father, in songs of everlasting praise:

Blessing and honour and glory and power be yours for ever and ever. Amen.

Pray for grace to live a Christian life and a useful one in the strength of the Blessed Sacrament.

Strengthen for service, Lord, the hands
    That holy things have taken;
Let ears that now have heard thy songs
    To clamour never waken.

Lord, may the tongues which 'Holy' sang
    Keep free from all deceiving;
The eyes which saw thy love be bright,
    Thy blessed hope perceiving.

The feet that tread thy holy courts
    From light do thou not banish;
The bodies by thy Body fed
    With thy new life replenish.

The readings and sermon, and the Sacrament itself, have spoken of Christ's way. Think again of their message. Pray for grace to walk in that way. You may like to make the Sign of the Cross as you say slowly and prayerfully:

May the grace of our Lord Jesus Christ, and the love of God, and the fellowship of the Holy Spirit, be with me now and always. Amen.